Pasta

The Taunton Press

ACADEMIA BARILLA
AMBASSADOR OF ITALIAN GASTRONOMY
THROUGHOUT THE WORLD

Academia Barilla is a global movement toward the protection, development and promotion of authentic regional Italian culture and cuisine.
With the concept of Food as Culture at our core, Academia Barilla offers a 360° view of Italy. Our comprehensive approach includes:

- a state-of-the-art culinary center in Parma, Italy;
- gourmet travel programs and hands-on cooking classes;
- the world's largest Italian gastronomic library and historic menu collection;
- a portfolio of premium artisan food products;
- global culinary certification programs;
- custom corporate services and training;
- team building activities;
- and a vast assortment of Italian cookbooks.

Thank you and we look forward to welcoming you in Italy soon!

CONTENTS

EDITED BY

ACADEMIA BARILLA

PHOTOGRAPHS

ALBERTO ROSSI

RECIPES BY

CHEF MARIO GRAZIA
CHEF LUCA ZANGA

TEXT BY

MARIAGRAZIA VILLA

ACADEMIA BARILLA EDITORIAL COORDINATION

CHATO MORANDI
ILARIA ROSSI
REBECCA PICKRELL

GRAPHIC DESIGN

PAOLA PIACCO

A WOMAN WHO KNOWS HOW TO MAKE PASTA TO PERFECTION HAS A PRESTIGE WHICH ENDURES EVEN TODAY, AGAINST ANY OTHER CALL OF THE TIMES.

SOPHIA LOREN, *IN CUCINA CON AMORE*, 1971

PASTA

It's the most Italian of pleasures. It is the symbol of a culture that celebrates not only the wisdom and creativity expressed at the stove, but also the joy of spending time together around the table. Pasta is a galaxy of gastronomy, an ever-new adventure of form, color, fragrance, style and flavor. It also breaks boundaries in cooking methods, history and accompaniments. There is no doubt that pasta has conquered the world, beginning in Italy, where it is practically a national monument to good living.

It seems that the Etruscans already had their hands in pasta, or, more accurately, in sheets of dough (as evidenced by the tools found around their tombs—the rolling pin and the wheel). The Romans knew of it (from Varro, who in the 1st century B.C. spoke of *lixulae*, ancestors to our gnocchi, to Apicius who, in the early years after Christ, described *lagane*, similar to our lasagna). And in Sicily during the late Middle Ages, we have the first historical record of artisanal and industrial production of dried pasta: in Trabia, near Palermo, where there continues to be a locally produced pasta called *itrya* (from the Arabic *itryah*, meaning a focaccia cut into strips). It was in the 1300s, however, that pasta began spreading to the other regions of Italy, and

the first pasta-producing companies were born. These were the same years that, hand in hand with pasta, the ancestor of the fork made its appearance. The *punctorio ligneo* was a pointed wooden utensil suggested for use in eating piping hot, slippery pasta, which was gaining widespread popularity. This, while the rest of Europe used their hands at the table until the 18th century.

Up until the 17th century, cookbooks referred to pasta as a side dish, particularly to meat, with a suggestion for cooking that would today be considered a bit overdone. Later pasta asserted itself as a dish in its own right. These days it has become more of a single-course meal, capable of providing not only carbohydrates, but also—owing to its sauces—proteins, good fats, and vegetables. And now it is cooked to *al dente*, just enough to maintain a pleasantly firm texture.

Finally, in the 18th century, with the first pasta makers and their rudimentary equipment, pasta became the Italian dish par excellence, synonymous with simplicity and goodness. Not a humble food, it is a delight to every palate, even the most refined. This is a sort of revenge by the ancient *genius loci* (spirit of place) in the sense that a diet structured around grains arises within the context of the Greco-Latin food culture, whereas nourishment based on meat or fish belongs to the Celto-Germanic tradition.

In Italian cuisine, pasta has virtually unlimited combinations. It can be fresh; filled or unfilled; kneaded with eggs, as done in the northern regions; or without, as in the south. And there are so many shapes that have been handed down by tradition, often to be used for feast days or holidays, and still made by hand in many areas of the country: from Bolognese tortellini to tagliolini of the Langhe in Piedmont; from Tuscan pappardelle to maccheroni alla chitarra from Abruzzi; from orecchiette of Puglia to cavatelli of Molise. Pasta can also be dried, with smooth or ribbed surfaces. Here also we can count an infinite variety of different shapes, whether long—linguine, spaghetti, or bucatini—or short—penne, fusilli, or farfalle. There are more than a hundred different types throughout the peninsula.

What about the sauces for dressing pasta? These are chosen according to the shape of the pasta and the type of occasion: the possibilities are truly endless. Ingredients, techniques, and cooking times can change: from classic Bolognese sauce with meat to timeless tomato sauce; from creamy cheese sauce to a light sauce of seafood or vegetables. The right sauce can make your pasta into a fresh summer salad or a warm winter delight.

We have collected 40 of the most inviting pasta recipes from the Italian tradition, selected by Academia Barilla, the international center dedicated to the preservation and promotion of Italian gastronomy. Some of these are typical of the *Bel Paese* ("the beautiful country," as Italians call their home) and are rightly famous throughout the world, such as Vermicelli with Tomato Sauce or alla Gricia, Rigatoni alla Norma, or all'Amatriciana, and Spaghetti Carbonara or or Spaghetti with Clams. But there are also lesser-known treasures, such as Trofie with Pesto and Tagliatelle with Bolognese Sauce. There are other pastas that arise from the successful pairing of traditional regional specialities: cheeses like ricotta or Pecorino; cured meats, such as speck, bresaola, or Parma ham; vegetables, like radicchio di Treviso, artichokes, eggplant, or asparagus; as well as truffles, balsamic vinegar from Modena, and on and on. These recipes all speak of the respect and love for the country's great raw materials and sophisticated techniques. But above all, their mission is to share the convivial spirit that belongs uniquely to pasta.

SEAFOOD BAVETTE

Preparation time: 40 minutes Cooking time: 8 minutes Difficulty: medium

4 SERVINGS

10 oz. (300 g) **bavette** (flat spaghetti) or fettucine
14 oz. (400 g) **mussels**
14 oz. (400 g) **clams**
4 **small red mullet**
4 **shrimp**
4 **prawns** (or jumbo shrimp)
5 oz. (150 g) **cherry tomatoes**, quartered

1 cup (150 ml) **white wine**
1 clove **garlic**, chopped
1 tbsp. (4 g) **parsley**, chopped
1 bunch **basil**, leaves torn
1 sprig **fresh oregano**
1/3 cup (80 ml) **extra-virgin olive oil**
Salt and pepper to taste

Remove oregano stem and chop leaves.
Throughly soak, clean and debeard the mussels and clams, rinsing well to remove all sand and grit.
Gut, fillet, and rinse the red mullet. Shell shrimp, leaving tail portion on, and devein.
Heat the olive oil in a skillet over medium and add the garlic, the parsley, the basil and the oregano.
Add the mussels, clams, and the white wine. Cover with a lid and let the mollusks open. When they have opened, remove them from the saucepan, shell three-quarters of them and place them in a bowl. In the same skillet, cook the red mullet, the whole prawns, the shelled shrimp and the quartered tomatoes.
Sauté for a few minutes, then add the mussels and the clams to the sauce.
Season it with salt and pepper to taste. When cooked, the sauce should be fairly liquid. In a pot of boiling salted water, cook the bavette until *al dente* (firm), drain, and then stir into the skillet with the sauce. Serve.

BAVETTE WITH JUMBO SHRIMP, MARSALA, AND SPRING ONIONS

Preparation time: 1 hour   Cooking time: 8 minutes   Difficulty: easy

4 SERVINGS

12 oz. (350 g) **bavette** (flat spaghetti) or fettucine

1 lb. (400 g) **jumbo shrimp**

2 1/2 oz. (70 g) **celery**, or about 2/3 cup chopped

3 oz. (85 g) **carrots**, or about 2/3 cup chopped

3 1/2 oz. (100 g) **onion**, or about 2/3 cup chopped

3 1/2 oz. (100 g) **spring onion**, or about 1 cup chopped

1 oz. (25 g) **tomato paste**, or about 1 1/2 tbsp

2 cloves **garlic**

3/4 cup plus 1 1/2 tbsp. (200 ml) **dry Marsala wine**

1/4 cup (60 ml) **extra-virgin olive oil**

4 1/2 cups (1 l) **water**

Salt and pepper to taste

Clean and shell the shrimp (reserving the shells) and cut shrimp into small pieces. Sauté the carrots, celery, and onion in a saucepan with half the oil and the 2 whole garlic cloves. After 5 minutes, add the shrimp shells and let them brown thoroughly. Then add the tomato paste and Marsala.

Let all the liquid evaporate, then pour in the water.

Season the sauce with salt and pepper and let simmer for 30 minutes.

Filter the sauce when it has cooked, and discard shrimp shells and solids. Saute the spring onion in the rest of the oil. Add the shrimp and season with salt and pepper. Slowly add the filtered sauce and let it cook for a few minutes.

Cook the pasta in a large pot of boiling salted water until *al dente*. Drain pasta and add it to the shrimp sauce. Cook pasta and sauce together for 1 minute, stirring well to combine. Serve.

BAVETTE WITH SWORDFISH
AND CHERRY TOMATOES

Preparation time: 1 hour   Cooking time: 8 minutes   Difficulty: easy

4 SERVINGS

11 oz. (300 g) **bavette** *(flat spaghetti) or fettucine*
11 oz. (300 g) **swordfish**, *medium diced*
11 oz. (300 g) **cherry tomatoes**, *halved*
3 tbsp. (45 ml) **extra-virgin olive oil**
1 clove **garlic**, *peeled*
Wild fennel frond
Chile pepper, *chopped*
Salt and pepper *to taste*

Heat half the oil in a nonstick pan, and sear the swordfish. Season with salt, pepper, and wild fennel to taste.

In a separate pan, heat the remaining oil and sauté whole garlic clove and the chile pepper. Add half the tomatoes, seasoned with salt to taste, and cook for a few minutes. Finally, add the fish.

Bring a pot of salted water to a boil and cook the pasta until *al dente*. Drain pasta and add it to the pan with the sauce. Cook together for a few seconds, mixing well, and serve.

BUCATINI ALL'AMATRICIANA

Preparation time: 15 minutes   Cooking time: 8 minutes   Difficulty: easy

4 SERVINGS

12 oz. (350 g) **bucatini**
6 oz. (150 g) **guanciale** *(pig's cheek) or* **pancetta**, *finely chopped*
4 ripe tomatoes
Crushed red pepper *to taste*
1/2 cup (40 g) **Pecorino Romano cheese**, *grated*
Salt and pepper *to taste*

Bring a large pot of salted water to a boil for the pasta.
Meanwhile, cut the guanciale or pancetta into slices and then into rectangles.
Add it to a pan over medium heat, along with a very small amount of water.
Simmer meat so that the fat melts.
In a saucepan of boiling water, blanch the tomatoes for 20 seconds, then cool and peel them, remove the seeds, and dice them.
Remove the guanciale or pancetta pieces from the pan and drain them thoroughly. Add the tomatoes to the pork fat in the pan. Season to taste with the crushed red pepper, salt and black pepper. Return the guanciale or pancetta pieces to the pan with the tomato sauce and heat briefly.
Cook the pasta in the pot of boiling water until *al dente*, drain, and dress with the sauce and the Pecorino. Mix well and serve hot.

BUCATINI
WITH PECORINO AND PEPPER

Preparation time: 10 minutes   *Cooking time: 6 minutes*   *Difficulty: easy*

4 SERVINGS

12 oz. (350 g) **bucatini**
7 tbsp. (100 ml) **extra-virgin olive oil**
7 oz. (200 g) **Pecorino Romano cheese**, *or about 2 cups, grated*
Coarsely ground black pepper *to taste*

Bring a large pot of salted water to a boil. Cook the pasta until *al dente*, and drain. Return the pasta to the pot and add the oil, Pecorino and black pepper to taste. The amount of black pepper can range from a light sprinkling to a generous handful. Mix well and serve immediately.

BUCATINI WITH CUTTLEFISH
AND PEAS

Preparation time: 30 minutes   Cooking time: 8 minutes   Difficulty: easy

4 SERVINGS

12 oz. (350 g) **bucatini**
12 oz. (350 g) **cuttlefish** (or squid)
7 oz. (200 g) **peas**, fresh or frozen, or
about 1 1/3 cup
4 oz. (150 g) **crushed tomatoes**
1 small **onion**

1 clove **garlic**
5-6 **fresh basil leaves**
7 tbsp. (100 ml) **dry white wine**
3 1/2 tbsp. (50 ml) **extra-virgin olive oil**
Salt to taste

Peel and chop the onion and garlic. Clean and rinse the cuttlefish, then cut it
into thin strips or very fine fillets, about 1/16 to 1/8 inch (2-3 mm) thick.
Drizzle a bit of olive oil in a pan and begin to sauté the onion and garlic.
Add the cuttlefish and cook for a few minutes, stirring constantly. Add the white
wine; when it has evaporated add the crushed tomatoes, peas and basil leaves.
Cook for 15 minutes more.
Meanwhile, bring a large pot of salted water to a boil and cook pasta until *al
dente*, drain, and transfer to a large bowl. Toss the pasta with the cuttlefish
sauce and serve hot.

CASTELLANE WITH ARTICHOKES
AND PECORINO

Preparation time: 45 minutes   Cooking time: 12 minutes   Difficulty: easy

4 SERVINGS

12 oz. (350 g) **castellane** (or penne rigate)
4 **artichokes**
2 oz. (60 g) **shallots**
2 oz. (60 g) **Pecorino cheese**, aged
3 1/2 tbsp. (50 ml) **dry white wine**
3 1/2 tbsp. (50 ml) **vegetable stock**

3 tbsp. (40 ml) **extra-virgin olive oil**
1 oz. (30 g) **parsley**, chopped
1 clove **garlic**
Juice of 1 **lemon**
Crushed red pepper
Salt to taste

Clean artichokes by slicing at least 1/4 inch (0.5 cm) off the tops and bottoms and removing all the tough outer leaves. Cut the artichokes in half lengthwise and remove the chokes. Cut into thin slices and soak in a bowl of water with the lemon juice to prevent the artichokes from turning black.
In a large skillet, gently sauté the artichoke slices in the oil, with the garlic, shallots, parsley, salt, chile to taste and the wine.
Cook until the wine evaporates, and then add a little of the stock and cook for about 10 more minutes.
In a pot of boiling salted water, cook the pasta until *al dente*.
Drain the pasta and add to the sauce. Shave the Pecorino into thin slices.
Garnish with the cheese.

CASTELLANE WITH DOGFISH
AND OLIVES

Preparation time: 15 minutes   Cooking time: 12 minutes   Difficulty: easy

4 SERVINGS

12 oz. (350 g) **castellane** *(or pasta shells)*
1 lb. (450 g) **dogfish** *(or halibut)*
7 oz. (200 g) **cherry tomatoes,** *or about 11 tomatoes*
2 oz. (50 g) **black olives,** *pitted, or about 11 large olives*
8 **pickled caperberries**
1 tbsp. (4 g) **minced parsley**
1 clove **garlic**
3 1/2 tbsp. (50 ml) **extra-virgin olive oil**
Salt and pepper *to taste*

In a large pan, sauté the entire garlic clove in half the olive oil. Dice the fish and add it to the pan, letting it cook for a few minutes. Cut the tomatoes into quarters and add them to the fish. Season with salt and pepper and cook for another 5 minutes. Rinse the caperberries and cut them in half, thinly slice the olives, and add them both to the pan. Remove the garlic and let the sauce simmer. In a small bowl or cup, mix the remaining olive oil with the minced parsley. Meanwhile, bring a large pot of salted water to a boil and cook the pasta until *al dente*. Drain the pasta and combine it with the dogfish sauce. Distribute it among serving plates and drizzle the olive oil–parsley mix over each portion.

CONCHIGLIONI
WITH SICILIAN-STYLE PESTO

Preparation time: 30 minutes   Cooking time: 12 minutes   Difficulty: easy

4 SERVINGS

12 oz. (350g) **conchiglioni** *(pasta shells)*
2 1/4 lb. (1 kg) **small plum tomatoes**, *preferably Piccadilly*
1/4 cup plus 2 tbsp. (50 g) **pine nuts**, *coarsely chopped*
1/2 cup (50 g) **coarsely chopped almonds**
1 **onion**, *chopped*
1 clove **garlic**, *peeled*
1/2 cup (120 g) **ricotta**
1 bunch **basil**, *chopped*
3 1/2 tbsp. (50 ml) **extra-virgin olive oil**
Salt, black pepper and crushed red pepper *to taste*

Peel the tomatoes, remove the seeds, and coarsely chop.
Heat the oil in a pan, and fry the onion until golden, along with the whole clove of garlic. Season to taste with a little crushed red pepper.
Add the almonds and pine nuts and cook for 2 minutes. Add the chopped tomatoes and season with salt and pepper. Cook for about 15 minutes, remove the garlic, then stir the ricotta into the sauce. Lastly, add the chopped basil.
Bring a pot of salted water to a boil and cook the conchiglioni until *al dente*; drain and dress with the pesto.

FARFALLE
WITH EGGPLANT SAUCE

Preparation time: 15 minutes   Cooking time: 12 minutes   Difficulty: easy

4 SERVINGS

12 oz. (300 g) **farfalle** *(bowtie pasta) or fusilli*
1 1/2 lb. (700 g) **eggplant**
2 tbsp. (30 ml) **extra-virgin olive oil**
1 bunch **basil**
Salt and pepper *to taste*

Bring a pot of salted water to a boil. Peel the eggplant (reserving some peel for garnish, if desired) and cut it into large pieces, then boil it for about 10 minutes or until softened.

Drain the eggplant and blend in a blender with the basil and a pinch of salt and pepper until a thick sauce forms. In a pot of boiling salted water, cook the pasta until *al dente*. While cooking the pasta, warm the eggplant sauce over medium heat, adding salt and pepper to taste.

Drain the pasta and add to the sauce. Add the olive oil and sauté the pasta. Stir again and serve in pasta dishes. As a garnish, lightly fry thinly sliced eggplant peels in the sauté oil.

FUSILLI WITH SALMON
AND CHERRY TOMATOES

Preparation time: 20 minutes   Cooking time: 12 minutes   Difficulty: easy

4 SERVINGS

12 oz. (300 g) **fusilli** (or penne)
1 lb. (450 g) **salmon fillets**, skinned and cubed
12 oz. (350 g) **cherry tomatoes**, halved
3 1/2 oz. (100 g) **onion**, roughly chopped
2 tbsp. (30 ml) **extra-virgin olive oil**
Salt and pepper to taste

Heat oil in a pan over low heat and sauté the onion for 2 minutes. Increase the heat to high and add the fish. Allow to brown for 2 minutes. Season with salt and pepper. Add the tomatoes. Reduce heat to medium and cook for an additional 5 minutes, adding water as needed to keep fish moist.
Season to taste with salt and pepper. Meanwhile, bring a large pot of salted water to a boil, and cook the pasta until *al dente*.
Drain the pasta and add it to the fish. Sauté for 1 minute while mixing with the sauce.

FUSILLI WITH SPECK
AND RADICCHIO

Preparation time: 20 minutes   Cooking time: 12 minutes   Difficulty: medium

4 SERVINGS

12 oz. (300 g) **fusilli** *(or sedani rigati)*
2 tbsp. (30 ml) **extra-virgin olive oil**
1/2 lb. (250 g) **radicchio**, *cut in strips*
1/4 lb. (120 g) **speck**, *cut in strips*
2/3 cup (150 ml) **heavy cream**
1 1/2 oz. (40 g) **shallots**, *sliced*
Salt and pepper *to taste*

Heat oil in a pan over low heat and sauté the shallots, letting them brown for 3 to 4 minutes. Reduce heat to medium, add the speck and sauté for another 2 to 3 minutes.
Add the radicchio and cook for 5 minutes.
Add the cream and season with salt and pepper.
Reduce the sauce, if necessary, over low heat.
Meanwhile, bring a large pot of salted water to a boil, and cook the pasta until *al dente*.
Drain the pasta and mix thoroughly with the sauce.

FUSILLI WITH ARUGULA PESTO

Preparation time: 15 minutes   Cooking time: 12 minutes   Difficulty: easy

4 SERVINGS

12 oz. (300 g) **fusilli** *(or farfalle [bowtie pasta])*
3 1/2 oz. (100 g) **arugula**
3/4 oz. (20 g) **Parmigiano-Reggiano cheese**, *grated, or about 4 tbsp.*
1 tbsp. (10 g) **pine nuts**
3/4 cups plus 1 1/2 tbsp. (200 ml) **extra-virgin olive oil**, *preferably Ligurian*
1/4 clove **garlic**
Salt *to taste*

Rinse and dry the arugula, then purée with 2/3 cup (150 ml) of oil, a pinch of salt,
the garlic and the pine nuts. Stir in the grated cheese. Cover with the remaining
oil and set aside.
Bring a large pot of salted water to a boil, and cook the pasta until *al dente*.
Add pasta to the pesto. Stir while diluting with a little cooking water and a
drizzle of oil.

GNOCCHI WITH RICOTTA

Preparation time: 15 minutes   Cooking time: 14 minutes   Difficulty: easy

4 SERVINGS

12 oz. (300 g) **semolina gnocchi** *(or medium shells)*
8 oz. (250 g) **very fresh ricotta cheese**
4 oz. (100 g) **peas**
2 oz. (60 g) **Pecorino cheese**, *grated, or about 2/3 cup*
Salt and pepper *to taste*

Cook the peas for 1 minute in a pot of boiling salted water, then drain and
plunge them into ice water to stop the cooking process.
Run the ricotta through a fine-mesh sieve into a large mixing bowl, then season
with a pinch of salt and pepper.
Bring a large pot of salted water to a boil, and cook the gnocchi until *al dente*.
Drain the gnocchi, set aside a little of the cooking liquid, and add the gnocchi to
the ricotta.
Stir in the grated cheese and the peas. Mix all the ingredients well.
If necessary, add a few tablespoons of the cooking water. Serve hot.

FUSILLI PASTA SALAD
WITH VEGETABLES AND SQUID

Preparation time: 15 minutes   *Cooking time: 12 minutes*   *Difficulty: medium*

4 SERVINGS

14 oz. (400 g) **fusilli pasta**
2 **carrots**, peeled
2 **zucchini**
2 **artichokes**
3 **squid**

1 bunch **aromatic herbs and greens**, such as basil and arugula
1/4 cup (60 ml) **extra-virgin olive oil**
Juice of 1 **lemon**
Salt and white pepper to taste
3 1/2 oz. (100 g) **Swiss chard**

Clean artichokes by slicing at least 1/4 inch (0.5 cm) off the tops and bottoms and removing the tough outer leaves. Cut artichokes in half lengthwise and remove the chokes. Cut into thin slices and soak in a bowl of water with 3 tablespoons of lemon juice to prevent artichokes from turning black.
Cut carrots and zucchini into matchsticks.
Clean the squid by cutting off the tentacles below the eyes. Flip the tentacles back and squeeze out and discard the beak. Trim off the "wings" on the sides of the body. Starting at the tip of the body, run the dull edge of the knife firmly down the squid to simultaneously peel off much of the membrane and squeeze out the viscera. Rinse the cleaned tentacles and bodies, inside and out. Cut squid into very thin strips.
Bring a large pot of salted water to a boil and cook the pasta. Five minutes before pasta reaches *al dente*, add the vegetables to the pasta pot. Stir and cook 3 minutes, then add the squid for the last 2 minutes. Drain pasta, add a little oil, transfer everything to a serving plate and let cool. When cool, dress with remaining oil and lemon juice. Season with salt and white pepper.
Serve on a bed of herbs and greens.

LINGUINE WITH FAVA BEANS, OLIVES AND HAKE

Preparation time: 50 minutes   Cooking time: 8 minutes   Difficulty: easy

4 SERVINGS

FOR THE PASTA
Vegetable broth *(recipe follows)*
12 oz. (350 g) **linguine**
8 oz. (250 g) **fresh fava beans**, or
about 1 1/3 cups
8 oz. (250 g) **hake fillets**, largely diced
2 oz. (50 g) **black olives**, or about 12
large, pitted and roughly chopped
1 oz. (30 g) **onion**, or about 1/2 small,
peeled
1 clove **garlic**, peeled
1 tbsp. (4 g) **parsley**, minced

3 tbsp. (40 ml) **extra-virgin olive oil**
Salt and pepper to taste

FOR THE VEGETABLE BROTH
2 1/2 oz. (75 g) **onion**, or about 1
small, peeled
2 cups (500 ml) **water**
1 1/2 oz. (40 g) **carrot**, or about 3/4
small, peeled
1 oz. (30 g) **celery**, or about 1 medium
stalk
Salt to taste

Make the vegetable broth by adding the whole vegetables to the cold water in a pot. Bring the water to a boil and let it boil for about 30 minutes, then strain it and set it aside. For the pasta, finely chop the onion and sauté it in the oil with the whole garlic clove until golden brown. Add the hake and season with salt and pepper. Blanch and peel the fava beans and add them to the sauce.
Add enough broth to cover everything and let it cook for 10 minutes.
Add the olives at the end.
Bring a large pot of salted water to a boil and cook the pasta until *al dente*.
Drain pasta and transfer it to the pan with the sauce. Cook together for a minute, mixing well. Garnish each serving with minced parsley, freshly ground pepper and a drizzle of olive oil.

MACCHERONCINI OR LINGUINE
WITH SHRIMP

Preparation time: 25 minutes   Cooking time: 12 minutes   Difficulty: medium

4 SERVINGS

12 oz. (350 g) **maccheroncini** *(or linguine)*
16 **medium shrimp**, *shelled and deveined*
3 1/2 oz. (100 g) **onion**, *or about 1 1/2 small*
8 oz. (250 g) **cherry tomatoes**, *or about 15*
3 1/2 tbsp. (50 ml) **brandy**
1 clove **garlic**, *peeled*
1 tbsp. (4 g) **parsley**, *minced*
5-6 **fresh basil leaves**, *torn*
3 tbsp. (40 ml) **extra-virgin olive oil**
Salt and pepper *to taste*

Cut each shrimp into 4 or 5 pieces. Quarter tomatoes and remove the seeds.
Chop the onion and garlic and sauté them in 2 tablespoons of the oil over low
heat until softened. Add the shrimp, increase heat to high and brown shrimp
for a few minutes. Carefully add the brandy and let it flambé.
Then add the tomatoes, parsley and basil.
Let it simmer for 10 minutes. Bring a large pot of salted water to a boil and cook
the maccheroncini until it is al dented. Drain pasta, combine it with the shrimp
sauce, and season to taste with salt and pepper. Finish with a drizzle of olive oil.

MEZZE MANICHE OR PENNE RIGATE
WITH SEAFOOD AND MUSHROOMS

Preparation time: 20 minutes   Cooking time: 14 minutes   Difficulty: easy

4 SERVINGS

12 oz. (300 g) **mezze maniche** (or penne rigate)
20 **medium shrimp**
5 oz. (150 g) **fresh tuna or swordfish**, cut into 1/2-inch (1.5 cm) cubes
8 oz. (200 g) **button mushrooms**, sliced
3 1/2 oz. (100 g) **tomatoes**, seeded and diced
1/4 cup (60 ml) **extra-virgin olive oil**
3/4 oz. (20 g) **parsley**, chopped, or about 1/3 cup
1 clove **garlic** peeled and chopped
Salt and pepper to taste

Shell the shrimp (leaving tail sections on, if desired), and devein. Bring a large pot of salted water to a boil, and cook the pasta until *al dente*.
Meanwhile, in a pan with 2 tbsp. of the oil, sear the tuna and shrimp for about 2 minutes. Season with salt and pepper and set aside.
In the same pan, add the remaining oil, sauté the garlic and, before it starts turning golden brown, add the mushrooms. Sauté for 2 minutes, then add the tomatoes. Continue cooking for another 2 minutes, adding a little of the pasta cooking water if needed. Add the shrimp and tuna. Drain the pasta and add it to the sauce. Add the parsley and sauté.

BUCATINI WITH SARDINES

Preparation time: 15 minutes   Cooking time: 15 minutes   Difficulty: medium

4 SERVINGS

14 oz. (400 g) **bucatini**
7 oz. (200 g) **sardines**
3 1/2 tbsp. (50 ml) **extra-virgin olive oil**
2 stalks **wild fennel**, *chopped*
3 cloves **garlic**
1 **onion**, *finely chopped*
3 oz. (80 g) **salt-packed anchovies**
(whole or filleted)

1 oz. (30 g) **raisins**, *or about 3 tbsp. packed*
1 oz. (30 g) **pine nuts**
1 tbsp. (4 g) **parsley**, *chopped*
1 pinch **saffron**
Dried breadcrumbs *as needed*
Salt and pepper *to taste*

Soak the raisins, covering them completely with lukewarm water for 20 minutes, then drain. Meanwhile, if using whole sardines, rinse, bone, and fillet them. Heat 2 tablespoons of oil in a skillet over medium heat. Add 2 whole peeled cloves of garlic, a few tablespoons of cold water, a pinch of saffron diluted in a drop of water and salt and pepper to taste. Cook for about 4 minutes, then add the sardines and cook for 5 minutes. Remove skillet from heat, remove the garlic cloves and set them aside. Crush the anchovies in a mortar with the parsley and a ladleful of lukewarm water to create a pesto.

Heat the remaining oil in a saucepan. Add the remaining clove of garlic and the onion and sauté until the onion starts to brown. Add the fennel, raisins, pine nuts and anchovy-and-parsley pesto, and cook the sauce over medium heat for 5 minutes. Meanwhile, bring a large pot of salted water to a boil and cook the bucatini until *al dente*. Drain pasta, then stir in the sauce and the sardines and transfer to a baking pan lined with parchment paper.

Sprinkle lightly with breadcrumbs. Bake for 5 minutes at 350°F (180°C).

PENNE WITH SQUASH
AND PANCETTA

Preparation time: 30 minutes   Cooking time: 8 minutes   Difficulty: easy

4 SERVINGS

12 oz. (300 g) **penne or farfalle** (bowties)
1 1/2 lb. (650 g) **butternut or acorn squash**, *peeled, seeded, and cut into 1/2-inch (1 cm) cubes*
8 oz. (200 g) **pancetta** (cured pork), *thinly sliced*
1 3/4 oz. (50 g) **onion**, *chopped*
1 3/4 tbsp. (25 g) **unsalted butter**
Fresh thyme, *a few springs*
Salt and pepper *to taste*

Place half the squash cubes, the onion and a pinch of salt in a pot of cold water, and bring to a boil, cooking until squash is tender, 15 to 20 minutes. Meanwhile, heat the oven to 300°F (150°C). Place the pancetta on a baking pan and let the meat crisp in the oven, about 15 minutes.

Drain the squash mixture and carefully purée it in a blender.

Melt the butter in a pan over medium heat and sauté the thyme. Add the remaining squash cubes and sauté until tender.

Season to taste with salt and pepper. Add squash purée to the cubed squash.

Bring a large pot of salted water to a boil and cook the pasta to *al dente*.

Drain the pasta, add to the sauce and sauté together. Serve in pasta dishes garnished with the pancetta and a sprig of thyme.

PENNE ALL'ARRABBIATA

Preparation time: 30 minutes   Cooking time: 11 minutes   Difficulty: easy

4 SERVINGS

12 oz. (300 g) **penne rigate** *(or tortiglioni)*
1 1/3 lbs. (600 g) peeled and diced **tomatoes**
2 tbsp. (30 ml) **extra-virgin olive oil**
3/4 oz. (20 g) **parsley**, *chopped, for garnish*
2 garlic **cloves**, *sliced*
Red chile pepper, *fresh or dried, to taste*
Salt *to taste*

Bring a large pot of salted water to a boil. Heat the oil in a large frying pan over medium heat. Sauté the garlic with the oil and chile to taste, but don't let it brown too much. (If you're using fresh hot pepper, you should seed and slice it, but if you are using a dried hot pepper, wear disposable gloves and crush it by hand, or use crushed red pepper flakes.)

Once the garlic and chile are slightly browned, add the tomatoes. Season with salt and cook over medium heat for 15 minutes, stirring occasionally.

Meanwhile, cook the pasta in the pot of boiling water until *al dente*, then drain. Toss the penne with the sauce and serve, garnished with parsley.

PENNE WITH ASPARAGUS

Preparation time: 30 minutes   Cooking time: 9 minutes   Difficulty: easy

4 SERVINGS

12 oz. (350 g) **penne** *(or mezze penne)*
1 lb. (450 g) **asparagus**
7 tbsp. (100 ml) **heavy cream**
3 1/2 oz. (100 g) **Parmigiano-Reggiano cheese**, *grated, or about 1 cup*
1 oz. (30 g) **shallots**, *sliced*
1 tbsp. plus 1 tsp. (20 ml) **extra-virgin olive oil**
2 cups (1/2 l) **water**

Remove the hard ends of the asparagus and cut all the stalks to the same length. Set aside the asparagus tips and slice the stalks.

Heat oil in a frying pan and gently sauté the shallots until brown. Add the asparagus slices to the shallots and sauté for 2 minutes. Cover with the water and cook for about 15 minutes. Salt lightly. Transfer asparagus mixture to a blender, and purée.

In a pan of boiling water, blanch the asparagus tips for 3 to 4 minutes, then plunge in ice water to stop the cooking process.

Bring a large pot of water to a boil, and cook the pasta until *al dente*, then drain. In a large pan, toss the pasta with the asparagus purée. Add the asparagus tips, the heavy cream and the cheese, stir together and cook over a low heat for 1 minute before serving.

PENNETTE WITH PUMPKIN
AND PANCETTA

Preparation time: 40 minutes   Cooking time: 30 minutes   Difficulty: easy

4 SERVINGS

14 oz. (400 g) **pennette** (or penne)
10 1/2 oz. (300 g) **pumpkin**, or about
2 1/2 cups diced
7 oz. (200 g) **smoked pancetta** (or
bacon), sliced 1/8 inch (3 mm) thick
1 yellow **onion**, quartered
1 tbsp. (4 g) **parsley**, minced

1 sprig **rosemary**
1 clove **garlic**
Balsamic vinegar to taste
1 1/2 tbsp. (20 ml) **extra-virgin olive oil**
water
Salt and pepper to taste

Cut the pumpkin in half with a serrated knife. Scrape out and discard seeds and
any loose fibers from inside pumpkin. Peel one half of the pumpkin and cut into
a 1/2-inch (1 cm) dice; set aside. Cut the other half of the pumpkin into smaller
sections, place in a large pot with quartered onion, a pinch of salt and enough
water to cover vegetables and cook until tender, about 25 minutes. Drain,
reserving cooking water. Let pumpkin cool, then scoop flesh from peel. Transfer
cooked pumpkin and onion to a blender and purée. If it is too dense, add a bit
of the cooking water. Cut the pancetta into thin strips. Mince the rosemary,
parsley, and garlic. Heat the oil in a pan and sauté the diced pumpkin until
tender. Season it with salt and pepper, remove from pan with a slotted spoon,
and set aside. Sauté the pancetta in the same pan. When the fat starts to brown,
add the garlic, rosemary and half the parsley and cook for 2 minutes.
Add the pumpkin purée and diced pumpkin.
Bring a pot of salted water to a boil and cook the pasta until *al dente*; drain.
Toss pasta with the sauce. Stir quickly, incorporating the diced pumpkin.
Top with parsley and a few drops of balsamic vinegar.

REGINETTE OR PAPARDELLE
WITH MUSHROOMS

Preparation time: 20 minutes   Cooking time: 9 minutes   Difficulty: easy

4 SERVINGS

12 oz. (300 g) **reginette** *(or papardelle)*
14 oz. (400 g) **mixed mushrooms**, *such as chanterelle, cremini, and oyster*
2 tbsp. (30 ml) **extra-virgin olive oil**
3/4 oz. (20 g) **parsley**, *chopped, or about 1/3 cup*
1 clove **garlic**, *chopped*
Salt and pepper *to taste*

Scrub and slice the mushrooms. Sauté the garlic and parsley in the oil. Add the mushrooms and cook for about 5 minutes, making sure that the mushrooms remain firm. Season with salt and pepper.
Bring a large pot of salted water to a boil. Cook the pasta until *al dente*; drain. Toss pasta with the mushrooms and cook over low heat for a few minutes before serving.

RIGATONI ALLA NORMA

Preparation time: 1 hour   Cooking time: 10 minutes   Difficulty: easy

4 SERVINGS

12 oz. (350 g) **rigatoni**
9 oz. (250 g) **eggplant**
1 3/4 oz. (50 g) **onion**, *peeled and chopped*
1 clove **garlic**, *peeled*
2 1/4 lbs. (1 kg) **tomatoes**, *seeded and diced (or canned tomatoes, preferably San Marzano)*
6 leaves **basil**
1 3/4 oz. (50 g) **grated salted ricotta**
Salt and pepper *to taste*
Flour *as needed*
2 tbsp. (30 ml) **extra-virgin olive oil**, *plus more for frying*

Dice the eggplant or cut it into sticks, then put it in a colander, salt it lightly and allow it to drain for about 30 minutes.

Heat 1/2 inch of oil in a frying pan until shimmering. Dredge eggplant in flour and fry it until tender.

Heat 2 tablespoons of oil in a saucepan and sauté onion with the whole clove of garlic. Add the tomatoes, season with salt and pepper and cook for about 10 minutes, then pass everything through a vegetable mill. Add the eggplant to the tomato sauce.

Bring a large pot of salted water to a boil and cook the rigatoni until *al dente*; drain. In a large bowl, toss pasta with the tomato sauce and eggplant. Top each serving with basil and ricotta.

SEDANI WITH PARMA HAM

Preparation time: 15 minutes   Cooking time: 12 minutes   Difficulty: easy

4 SERVINGS

11 oz. (300 g) **sedani rigati pasta** *(or penne rigate)*
4 oz. (120 g) **Parma ham**, *cut in strips 1/10 inch (3 mm) thick*
3 1/2 tbsp. (50 g) **butter**
1 1/2 oz. (40 g) **Parmigiano-Reggiano cheese**, *shaved*
3 tbsp. (40 ml) **balsamic vinegar**, *preferably of Modena*
4 **sprigs of thyme**
Salt *to taste*

Bring a large pot of salted water to a boil. Meanwhile, melt the butter in a nonstick frying pan. Add the ham and allow to brown for 2 minutes; sprinkle with the balsamic vinegar and continue cooking for 3 to 4 minutes, so that the sauce has the consistency of a light syrup. Cook the pasta until *al dente*; drain. Remove leaves from sprigs of thyme and toss them with the pasta and the sauce in a large bowl.
Serve in pasta dishes and garnish with slivers of Parmigiano.

SPACCATELLE WITH MUSHROOMS,
BRESAOLA AND ARUGULA

Preparation time: 50 minutes   Cooking time: 9 minutes   Difficulty: easy

4 SERVINGS

12 oz. (300 g) **spaccatelle pasta** *(or casarecce or penne)*
7 oz. (200 g) **button mushrooms**, *trimmed and sliced, plus more for garnish*
3/4 cup plus 1 1/2 tbsp. (200 ml) **heavy cream**
3 1/2 oz. (100 g) **bresaola**, *cut in thin strips*
3 1/2 oz. (100 g) **tomatoes**, *diced*

1 3/4 oz. (50 g) **arugula**, *coarsely chopped, plus more for garnish*
1 1/2 oz. (40 g) **Parmigiano-Reggiano cheese**, *shaved*
2 tbsp. (30 ml) **extra-virgin olive oil**
1/3 cup (20 g) **parsley**, *chopped*
1 clove **garlic**, *peeled*
Salt and pepper *to taste*

Bring a large pot of salted water to a boil for pasta.
Heat a pan with the oil over medium heat. Sauté the garlic, mushrooms and parsley for 2 minutes. Season with salt and pepper.
Add the bresaola, then add the tomatoes. Cook for 5 minutes over high heat.
Add the cream, then reduce the heat to medium-low and let the sauce reduce for 2 to 3 minutes. Season with salt and pepper.
Meanwhile, cook the pasta until *al dente*; drain. Toss the pasta with the sauce and the arugula and sauté for a few minutes. Garnish with cheese and a few leaves of uncooked arugula or cooked mushroom slices.

SPAGHETTI CARBONARA

Preparation time: 10 minutes   Cooking time: 8 minutes   Difficulty: easy

4 SERVINGS

12 oz. (350 g) **spaghetti**
5 1/3 oz. (150 g) **guanciale** (pork cheek) or bacon
4 large **egg yolks**
3 1/2 oz. (100 g) **Pecorino Romano cheese**, *grated, or about 1/3 cup plus 1 tbsp.*
Salt and pepper *to taste*

Bring a large pot of salted water to a boil.
Beat the egg yolks in a bowl with a pinch of salt and a little Pecorino. Cut the guanciale or bacon into thin strips, about 1/12 inch (2 mm) thick, or into a small dice. Sauté with the oil over medium heat in a large saucepan.
Cook the spaghetti in the boiling water until *al dente*; drain, reserving some of the cooking water. Put the spaghetti in the skillet with the guanciale or bacon and toss together. Remove from the heat and add the egg yolks and a little cooking water, and mix for about 30 seconds. Mix in the remaining Pecorino and a grinding of black pepper, and serve immediately.

SPAGHETTI WITH CLAMS

Preparation time: 20 minutes   Cooking time: 8 minutes   Difficulty: easy

4 SERVINGS

12 oz. (350 g) **spaghetti**
2 1/4 lbs. (1 kg) **clams**
6 3/4 tbsp. (100 ml) **extra-virgin olive oil**
1 tbsp. (4 g) **parsley**, *chopped*
1 clove **garlic**, *chopped*
Salt and pepper *to taste*

Bring a large pot of salted water to a boil.
Scrub and rinse the clams thoroughly under running water. Place them in a large
skillet with 1 tablespoon of oil over medium heat. Cover with a lid and cook
them until they open (2 to 3 minutes), discarding any clams that do not open.
Remove the skillet from heat and shell half of the clams. Strain the cooking liquid
and pour it back into the skillet with the clams for the sauce. Set aside.
In another skillet, sauté the garlic in the remaining oil until golden brown. Add
the clams and the sauce and cook until it comes to a boil.
Meanwhile, cook the spaghetti in the boiling water until *al dente*; drain, reserving
some of the cooking water. Toss spaghetti with clams and sauce, adding cooking
water as needed. Sprinkle generously with pepper and chopped parsley.

SPAGHETTI WITH RADICCHIO
AND KING PRAWNS TARTARE

Preparation time: 15 minutes   Cooking time: 8 minutes   Difficulty: easy

4 SERVINGS

12 oz. (350 g) **spaghetti**

FOR THE SAUCE
3 tbsp. (40 ml) **extra-virgin olive oil**
1/4 cup (50 ml) **white wine**
2 oz. (60 g) **onion**, minced, or about *1/3 cup*
12 oz. (300 g) **radicchio**, preferably Treviso

1 clove **garlic**, minced
1 tbsp. (4 g) **minced parsley**
Salt and pepper to taste

FOR THE TARTARE
16 **king prawns or jumbo shrimp**
2 tsp. (10 ml) **extra-virgin olive oil**
Salt and pepper to taste

Bring a large pot of salted water to a boil.

Rinse the radicchio and cut it into strips. Drizzle some oil into a pan over medium heat and sauté the onion for 2 minutes. Add the garlic and radicchio and let the mixture cook for another 2 minutes. Add the wine and let cook until the radicchio has wilted. Season with salt and pepper.

Meanwhile, peel and devein the prawns.

Chop them finely, put them in a bowl, and mix well with a pinch of salt and pepper and a tablespoon of olive oil.

Cook the spaghetti in the boiling water until *al dente*; drain and immediately toss it with the radicchio, adding the parsley and a drizzle of olive oil. Divide the spaghetti among individual serving plates and top each with a spoonful of the prawns tartare. Sprinkle them with ground black pepper and a pinch of minced parsley, and finish with a drizzle of olive oil.

WHOLE-GRAIN SPAGHETTI
WITH PRAWNS

Preparation time: 20 minutes   Cooking time: 15 minutes   Difficulty: medium

4 SERVINGS

12 oz. (300 g) **whole-grain spaghetti** *(or bavette)*
12 **prawns** *(or jumbo shrimp), peeled and deveined*
7 oz. (200 g) **cherry tomatoes**, *cut in wedges*
1/4 cup (60 ml) **extra-virgin olive oil**
2 tbsp. (30 ml) **white wine**
1 oz. (30 g) **parsley**, *chopped*
1 clove **garlic**, *peeled*
1 small **red chile pepper**, *seeded and chopped*
Salt *to taste*

Bring a large pot of salted water to a boil.
Sauté the garlic in half the oil until golden brown. Add the chile and the prawns.
Sear quickly then add the wine. Once the wine has evaporated, add the
tomatoes and cook for 5 minutes. Season with salt and add the parsley.
Meanwhile, cook the pasta in the boiling water until *al dente*; drain, reserving
some of the cooking water.
Toss pasta with the prawns and sauté. Add a little of the pasta cooking water
and the remaining oil, and stir to combine.

TAGLIATELLE ALLA BOLOGNESE

Preparation time: 1 1/2 hours
Cooking time: 15 minutes   Difficulty: medium

4 SERVINGS

FOR THE TAGLIATELLE
2 1/2 cups (300 g) **all-purpose flour**
or Italian "00" type flour
3 large **eggs**

FOR THE SAUCE
2/3 cup (160 ml) **water**
5 oz. (150 g) **pork shoulder**, chopped
5 oz. (150 g) **ground beef**
5 oz. (150 g) **lard**

1 1/2 oz. (40 g) **carrots**
1 1/2 oz. (40 g) **celery**
1 1/2 oz. (40 g) **yellow onions**
3 oz. (90 g) **tomato paste**
1/2 cup (100 ml) **red wine**
6 3/4 tbsp. (100 ml) **extra-virgin olive oil**
2 bay **leaves**
1 1/2 oz. (40 g) grated **Parmigiano-Reggiano cheese**
Salt and pepper to taste

For the tagliatelle, place the flour on a clean work surface and make a well in the center. Add the eggs to the well, and gradually mix with the flour, kneading until the dough is smooth. Wrap the dough in lightly oiled plastic wrap and refrigerate for about 30 minutes. Using a rolling pin or pasta machine, roll the dough out into thin sheets, about 1/25 inch (1 mm) thick. Cut sheets into 1/4-inch-wide (6-7mm) strips. Spread them on a lightly floured work surface.
Chop all the vegetables. In a large pan over medium heat, sauté the lard. Add the vegetables and the bay leaves and cook until vegetables are golden brown. Add the beef and pork and sauté over a high flame. Add the red wine and cook until it evaporates. Reduce heat to low, add the tomato paste, salt and pepper and simmer sauce for about 1 hour, adding 1 or 2 tablespoons of water, if necessary. Bring a large pot of salted water to a boil and cook the tagliatelle until *al dente*; drain. In a large bowl, toss the tagliatelle with the sauce. Sprinkle with the Parmigiano-Reggiano, mix well and serve.

TAGLIOLINI WITH TRUFFLES

Preparation time: 40 minutes   Cooking time: 10 minutes   Difficulty: medium

4 SERVINGS

FOR THE TAGLIOLINI
2 1/2 cups (300 g) **all-purpose flour** or Italian "00" type flour
3 large **eggs**

FOR THE SAUCE
1/2 stick (50 g) **unsalted butter**
1 small **black truffle**
Salt to taste

For the tagliolini, place the flour on a clean work surface and make a well in the center. Add the eggs to the well, and gradually mix with the flour, kneading until the dough is smooth. Wrap the dough in lightly oiled plastic wrap and refrigerate for about 30 minutes.

Using a rolling pin or pasta machine, roll the dough out into thin sheets, about 1/25 inch (1 mm) thick. Cut into 1/10-inch-wide (2 mm) strips.

Bring a large pot of salted water to a boil. Cook the pasta until *al dente*. Drain, reserving some of the cooking water. Melt the butter in a saucepan and add about 1/2 cup of reserved cooking water.

Toss the pasta with the butter–cooking water mixture.

Put the pasta on serving plates and shave the truffle over the top just before serving.

TONNARELLI WITH SHRIMP

Preparation time: 1 hour   Cooking time: 5 minutes   Difficulty: medium

4 SERVINGS

FOR THE TONNARELLI
2 1/2 cups (300 g) **all-purpose flour** or
Italian "00" type flour
1/3 cup plus 2 tbsp. (75 g) **fine semolina**
3 large **eggs**
3 1/2 tbsp. (50 ml) **white wine**

FOR THE SAUCE
12 **jumbo shrimp**, shelled and deveined
5 oz. (150 g) **plum tomatoes**, seeded

2 tbsp. (30 ml) **white wine**
1 1/2 oz. (40 g) **toasted slivered
almonds**, or about 1/3 cup
1/4 cup (60 ml) **extra-virgin olive oil**
1 **red chile pepper**, seeded and sliced
into rounds
1 clove **garlic**
1 tbsp. (4 g) **parsley**, minced
Salt and pepper to taste

For the tonnarelli, place the flour on a clean work surface and make a well in the
center. Add the eggs and wine to the well, and gradually mix with the flour,
kneading until the dough is smooth. Wrap the dough in lightly oiled plastic wrap
and refrigerate for 30 minutes. Roll out dough to 1/16 inch (2 mm) thick and cut into
pieces to fit a *chitarra*, a guitar-like tool for making pasta (or use a special
attachment to your pasta maker). Let dough dry for a minute, then place a sheet of
dough over the strings of the chitarra and press down with a rolling pin. Place the
resulting tonnarelli on a baking sheet sprinkled with semolina. Don't overlap. Bring
a pot of salted water to a boil. Heat the whole garlic clove with half the oil. When
garlic turns golden, add the shrimp. Sear shrimp and add the white wine, cooking
until it evaporates. Add tomatoes and chile pepper. Cook for 3 minutes, season
with salt and pepper and add the parsley. Cook the pasta until *al dente*; drain. Toss
with the shrimp and sauce in the pan. Add remaining oil. Cook for 1 minute, mixing
well. Divide pasta among serving plates and top with the toasted almonds.

WHOLE-GRAIN TORTIGLIONI
WITH GOAT CHEESE AND SUN-DRIED TOMATOES

Preparation time: 10 minutes   Cooking time: 11 minutes   Difficulty: easy

4 SERVINGS

12 oz. (350 g) **whole-grain tortiglioni** *(or penne rigate)*
7 oz. (200 g) **fresh goat cheese**, *preferably Caprino*
2 oz. (60 g) **sun-dried tomatoes**, *cut in thin strips*
3/4 oz. (20 g) **green olives**, *pitted and chopped*
1 tbsp. plus 1 tsp. (10 g) **salted capers**
1 tbsp. plus 1 tsp. (20 ml) **extra-virgin olive oil**
2 or 3 **basil leaves**, *roughly torn*
Dried oregano and salt *to taste*

Bring a large pot of salted water to a boil and cook the pasta until *al dente*;
drain. Meanwhile, rinse the capers under running water, drain and chop coarsely.
Put the goat cheese in a large bowl and dilute with about 1/2 cup of the pasta
cooking water, then whisk until creamy. Add the capers, olives and tomatoes.
Season with salt and a pinch of oregano.
Add pasta to the goat cheese mixture, mix well. Add olive oil and basil and stir
well to combine.

TORTIGLIONI WITH ARTICHOKES,
PROSCIUTTO AND PECORINO

Preparation time: 15 minutes   Cooking time: 8 minutes   Difficulty: easy

4 SERVINGS

12 oz. (350 g) **whole-wheat tortiglioni**
(or penne rigate)
4 **artichokes**
Juice of 1 **lemon**
5 oz. (150 g) **sliced prosciutto**
3 oz. (80 g) **Pecorino Toscano cheese**,
shaved

3 1/2 tbsp. (50 ml) **extra-virgin olive oil**
1 sprig **rosemary**
1 clove **garlic**
1 **onion**, sliced
Salt and pepper to taste

Clean artichokes by slicing at least 1/4 inch (0.5 cm) off the tops and bottoms and removing and discarding all the tough outer leaves. Set tender inner leaves aside. Cut artichokes in half lengthwise and remove the chokes. Cut the hearts in half, removing any tough parts, slice thinly and soak in a bowl of water with the lemon juice to prevent artichokes from turning black. Heat a pan with 2 tablespoons of oil over medium heat. Sauté onion slices until translucent. Add artichoke leaves and enough water to cover ingredients. Braise for about 30 minutes, or until leaves are tender. In a blender, purée artichoke leaves and onions and pass them through a fine-mesh strainer. Bring a pot of salted water to a boil and cook pasta until *al dente*. Meanwhile, cut the prosciutto into strips and chop rosemary leaves and garlic. In a pan with the remaining oil over medium heat, brown the sliced artichoke hearts. Add prosciutto, rosemary, garlic and salt and pepper to taste. Cook for another 2 minutes, adding the strained artichoke purée toward the end. Toss cooked pasta with artichoke sauce in the pan and cook for 1 minute. Transfer to serving plates and top with shaved Pecorino and remaining 1 tbsp. of olive oil.

TRENETTE WITH ZUCCHINI
AND SMOKED SWORDFISH

Preparation time: 15 minutes   Cooking time: 8 minutes   Difficulty: easy

4 SERVINGS

12 oz. (300 g) **trenette** *(or spaghettini)*
7 oz. (200 g) **zucchini,** *julienned*
1 oz. (30 g) **shallots,** *chopped*
6 oz. (160 g) **smoked swordfish**
2 tbsp. (30 ml) **extra-virgin olive oil**
3/4 oz. (20 g) **parsley,** *chopped, or about 1/3 cup*
Zest of 1/2 **lemon**
Salt and pepper *to taste*

Bring a large pot of salted water to a boil.
Cut the swordfish into matchsticks.
Heat the oil in a pan and sauté the shallots over medium heat, until just golden brown. Raise the heat to medium-high and add the zucchini. Sauté for 1 minute, season with salt and pepper and remove from heat.
Add the fish and the lemon zest to the pan and stir.
Cook the pasta in the pot of boiling water until *al dente*; drain, reserving some of the cooking water and add immediately to the sauce over low heat. Sauté, adding the parsley and, if necessary, a little of the cooking water.

TROFIE WITH PESTO

Preparation time: 1 hour   Cooking time: 5 minutes   Difficulty: medium

4 SERVINGS

FOR THE TROFIE
2 1/2 cups (300 g) **all-purpose flour** or
Italian "0" type flour
2/3 cup (150 ml) **water**
This recipe can also be prepared with
14 oz. (400 g) of **ready-made trofie**

FOR THE SAUCE
1 oz. (30 g) **basil**
1/2 oz. (15 g) **pine nuts**

2 oz. (60 g) **Parmigiano-Reggiano
cheese**, grated, or about 2/3 cup
1 1/3 oz. (40 g) **aged Pecorino cheese**,
grated, or about 1/3 cup plus 1 tbsp.
1 clove **garlic**
3 1/2 oz. (100 g) **green beans**
7 oz. (200 g) **potatoes**, peeled and diced
6 3/4 oz. (200 ml) **extra-virgin olive oil**,
preferably Ligurian
Salt to taste

Mound the flour on a clean work surface, creating a well in the center. Knead with sufficient water to make a firm, elastic dough. Cover the dough with plastic wrap and let it rest for 30 minutes. Break off chickpea-sized pieces of dough and roll them in your hands (or on the work surface, pressing down lightly at the same time) to make the trofie. Rinse the basil and dry it well. In a mortar, crush the basil, pine nuts and the peeled clove of garlic with 5 ounces (150 ml) olive oil, a pinch of salt and the grated cheese. Alternatively, pulse the ingredients in a blender or food processor until well mixed. Pour resulting pesto into a bowl and cover with the remainder of the olive oil. Boil the potatoes and green beans until crisp-tender. When the vegetables are almost cooked, add the pasta to the same pot and cook for about 4 minutes. (For ready-made pasta, cook per package instructions for *al dente*.) Remove from the heat and drain. Toss with the pesto, diluting with a little cooking water and a drizzle of extra-virgin olive oil.

VERMICELLI
WITH TOMATO SAUCE

Preparation time: 30 minutes   Cooking time: 13 minutes   Difficulty: easy

4 SERVINGS

11 oz. (300 g) **vermicelli** *(or spaghetti)*
1 1/3 lbs. (600 g) **tomatoes**, *peeled and diced*
3 1/2 oz. (100 g) **onion**, *chopped*
2 tbsp. (30 ml) **extra-virgin olive oil**
8 **basil leaves**, *coarsely chopped*
1 garlic **clove**, *peeled*
Salt and pepper *to taste*

Heat the oil in a frying pan over medium. Fry the onion and garlic until golden brown. Add the tomatoes and season with salt and pepper. Raise heat to high and cook for about 20 minutes, stirring occasionally.
Meanwhile, bring a large pot of salted water to a boil.
Remove the garlic and add the basil to the onion-tomato mixture.
Cook the pasta until *al dente* in the boiling water; drain.
Toss the pasta with the sauce and serve.

VERMICELLI ALLA GRICIA

Preparation time: 10 minutes   Cooking time: 13 minutes   Difficulty: easy

4 SERVINGS

11 oz. (300 g) **vermicelli** (or bucatini)
5 oz. (150 g) **cured pork cheek** (guanciale) or bacon, medium dice
3 1/2 tbsp. (50 ml) **extra-virgin olive oil**
1 1/2 oz. (40 g) **Pecorino Romano cheese**, grated, or about 1/3 cup plus 1 tbsp
Salt, black pepper and crushed red pepper to taste

Sauté the meat in the oil over medium heat for 3 minutes. Add crushed red peper to taste. Meanwhile, bring a large pot of salted water to a boil and cook the pasta until *al dente*. Drain the pasta and toss it in the pan with the meat. Sprinkle with grated cheese and freshly ground black pepper to taste.

INGREDIENTS INDEX

PHOTO CREDITS

All photographs are by ACADEMIA BARILLA except the following:
pages 6, 95 ©123RF